your healing is today

D1547973

I recently visited someone in the hospital who was paralyzed, who could not move, sit up or walk. She had been advised by her doctors that she must have an immediate operation or she would never walk again. She refused. We worked together with the principles of Mind as set forth in this book, knowing her as being an individualization of Life, of God. We were actively aware of her perfection, wholeness, completeness NOW. I visited her two days later and she was sitting up in bed. We again gave ourselves up to a complete idea, knowing instantaneous results. I returned to the hospital two days later and she had already gone home. Healed.

Tom Johnson

LOS ARBOLES PUBLICATIONS
P.O. Box 7000-54
Redondo Beach, California 90277

11/95

your healing is today

TREATMENT, or scientific prayer, is a deliberate and definite mental technique which we can use to lift the consciousness or state of mind to such a high and dynamic level that we contact that area of mind in which God thinks. As this is accomplished, the individual who does it permits the power of pure life, God, to flow into his own individual use of life, his own individual use of thought. It is the law of mind that at whatever level of thought we function, our way of thought is accepted without question into the great medium, subconscious mind, and this use of thought then becomes experience, form, body, our individual outer worlds. Since all thought is creative, it is imperative that we find the highest possible way to direct this precise and infallible law of mind.

There is everywhere present a Thinker, a Life, a Power, a Presence, that is absolute, complete, perfect, infinite, total. Since we can use our thought consciously and deliberately, we can choose to use it to be aware of this wholeness, this completeness, this Infinite Thinker. We can become at one with It simply by directing our thought to this Being. We can identify with this concept of completeness, which, after all, is a way of thought. As we accomplish this, to whatever degree, this total way of thought instantly is our now experience. There is no law which says that we cannot think in a certain way. Change your thought and you instantly feel something new. A new experience begins right away.

What you are now thinking is certainly more important than what you have been thinking, and it is also more important than what you will eventually be thinking, for your now use of thought is your point of control. It is actually your present experience because it brings you into a state of mind, a mood, a level of consciousness, which in turn, immediately changes your outer world. Change your thought and you instantly change your experience. You can do this deliberately because you are always free to think whatever you choose. As we move along we shall see that we must always use our thought consciously and deliberately so that we can be free of fear, worry, problems, the domination or influence of someone else's use of thought.

The purpose of our conscious use of thought, treatment, is not to make something new happen. It is not so that we will eventually have the demonstration or manifestation of whatever it is that we desire. Our purpose in treatment is to rise in our use of thought to a full recognition, an acceptance and awareness, that Life already is, God already is, that Wholeness already is. We must use our thought to be aware that health already is. If God is that which is perfect, total, and complete, and It is, then God is that experience which we can label health. If there were no such thing as health, then one could not believe in God, for the awareness of God must produce health. Since God is life, since we are all aware of this Presence when we choose to be aware of It, then we cannot refute God, we cannot refute Life, we cannot refute health. In other words, treatment is for the purpose of becoming aware of that which already is, and in our awareness of all that is, the law of mind is instantly directed in this larger way, thereby freeing that which already is to be our now experience. In realizing that this is the way mind works, we have a way to bring about instantaneous healing, a complete freedom from the pains and the aches which result from believing falsely in the power of body.

We can select any way to think that we desire, and if we choose to always be looking at body by means of our thought, being aware of body, then **this** way of thought must be our instantaneous experience. Whatever you are aware of, whether it be a memory, something that is visible or invisible (such as a belief, an idea), your use of thought instantly creates a mood, a state of mind. You can become depressed in a moment simply because you have unconsciously chosen to think in the wrong way. You have unwittingly given your attention to a negative idea, to a wrong interpretation of life. You always find what you look for. The thing that you look for is the thing that you look with. In other words, what you really seek is a state of mind, an idea. You can become filled with joy in an instant because you give your attention to a beautiful idea, to one of success, of greatness. Your use of thought leads and body instantly follows. All that you think affects your body immediately.

As you take charge of your thought and become more completely aware of the power with which you are working, you can use your thought to become more aware of the fullness, the completeness, that already is. As you take your attention away from the physical appearance and deliberately put it on the spiritual identity of yourself or of the person for whom you are treating, this awareness of wholeness becomes the now experience. Before you can do this for others, however, you must first of all be able to do it for yourself. We must never in our study of the science of mind discover how thought works merely to have someone else use their thought for us. They can certainly do so, and there might be the time when it is essential, but being able to use our thought for ourselves is the goal. Being self-sufficient is our goal, our purpose. Since it is the law of mind that whatever way of thought is used, whoever thinks it experiences it, you cannot really know something for someone else without being aware of it for yourself first of all, thus experiencing it yourself in some individual way. You always must reap what you put into mind, regardless of who you are thinking about or for. You can think about whatever you desire.

Treatment is the art of turning away in thought from that which appears to be and using thought deliberately and specifically to be aware of the completeness and perfection of life so that the law of mind is directed in a total way. This new way of thought automatically results in what the world calls a healing, but it is really revelation of, or the experience of, the Whole Self, the experience of God.

Each one of us was created in the image and likeness of Life, which is God. Since God is not a physical body or **any** kind of form, but is that which is everywhere present at all times in Its entirety, then we were all created in the image and likeness of Life, Wholeness, Completeness. God already is. We do not have to use our thought to make God happen, to make Life live, or to make health be. Life already is. Too often in our treatments we are telling Life to be life in a particular way, but Life is already Life as the perfection of God. Is it not rather presumptuous on our part to think that we know more than all of Life, than all of God? In directing our thought in this egotistical way, we are trying to correct body with our thought instead of leaving this manifestation of wholeness up to an intelligence that knows exactly what to do and how to do it. If we give our attention to the verdicts of the doctor, or to the bandages or pains or agonized expressions of fear, we are certainly not thinking at the level of God. We are, rather, believing in the absence of God. A belief in the idea of cancer is really a disbelief in the Presence of God. This does not mean in any way that there is no God. It simply means that you do not believe in the totality of God. Any belief in a power apart from completeness or wholeness directs the law of mind to attain and maintain a negative or limited experience. You are always the experience of your thought.

Your healing can be today, NOW, when you rise above the level of appearances, when you see beyond the conflicts, confusions, fears, and doubts of others and, instead, deliberately use your thought to become at one with a higher level of consciousness wherein none of these exist. In the Mind of God, in this complete way of thought, there simply cannot be thoughts of disease, poverty, or failure, for the Infinite Thinker can only think that which is Infinite. It can only be aware of perfection, of completeness. God is a way of thought emanating from Its self-awareness. God is a way of thought that realizes Who and

What It really is. If, after all, there were thoughts of death being used at the level of God, then the law of mind would have taken these thoughts and produced the experience of death for God, for Life, and none of us would exist. If this were so, then there would be no life—there would only be death. There is no such thing as *belief* death because death is only a false idea in the mind of man. God does not know death. Life does not know death.

Since you and I are each an individualization of life, none of us can ever really die. We merely experience the degree of life that is brought about by our way of thought—nothing more, nothing less. There is always something that you can do about your thought. We can never, however, get away from the Truth that Life already is. There is no such thing as a part of Life, a small degree of Life. Life is that which is complete, Infinite, unlimited. It always has been and It always will be. As we are aware of it, as we believe in It, we **are** It. You can have your instantaneous healing when you are at one with Life. This means releasing yesterday and tomorrow in your use of thought, for **Today** is where Life is.

Today is God. When you rise in consciousness to the NOW, wherein God resides, you experience wholeness at the level of mind and body.

If you were to become emotionally involved with the suffering of a friend, regardless of his problem, you would actually be involving yourself with a way of thought, which is really the essence of any experience. Should you enter into his way of thought, his state of mind, you would find yourself involved with his fears of tomorrow or his resentments of yesterday. You would be a part of fear, anxiety, anger, resentment, worry, hate, some way of thought indicating a separation from the total, complete Self that each of us really is. If this were the case, you would be neither helping yourself nor anyone else, for sympathy never helps anyone to be aware of fullness, of Life, of freedom. In sympathizing, you are, in effect, believing in a problem and directing the law of mind in a distorted way against yourself as well as your friend. What you give your attention to you must experience yourself. Something instantly happens in an individual way for you as well. It may result in a mood of depression or anxiety, and this will affect your body in some appropriate way, such as lack of energy, loss of appetite (or even an increase in food intake), or loss of sleep. The normal pattern is thrown out of kilter in some immediate way.

The science of God-awareness had to come into being because so many people have been using their thought in the wrong way, and so many are searching for a way to be free. The wrong use of thought has been taught to practically all of us from the time we came into this particular plane of expression, and it has created so many problems, so much unhappiness and disease, that the revelation of a way to freedom had to be revealed. The desire caused the law of mind to reveal the way. The law of mind has always been. No one created it. No one prayed for a law of mind. It has always been and always will be.

Effective treatment is possible because of our discovery of the nature of thought to become form. In simply being aware of the law of mind, we are aware of the power of our word. Power has always been within the word, in however we choose to think. Since we always experience what we believe, we must give careful attention to selecting the ideas we use. If you choose to believe in disease, then this is what you must experience. If you choose to believe in God, this is what you must experience. If you choose to believe in instantaneous healing, this must be your experience. If you think at the level of the power, the life, the perfection that already is, this must be your now experience. It is all a matter of becoming aware. Treatment is being aware of that which already is. It is not trying to force something into our experience, it is not trying to create something.

If you desire something, and it is always the **experience** of an idea that you desire, this means that it already is, or you would not be able to be aware of it. If it is in Mind, it is. Being aware of it releases it into your experience. The more you are aware, the more quickly it is your experience. The more you believe in instantaneous healing, the more you demonstrate instantaneous healing. We must go all the way with our thought. We must go right to the Source, to the wholeness that already is. Healing is not something that is going to be.

It is something that is. It is the revelation of a completeness that has always been and always will be. It is right now. We must use our thought to be at one with the NOW, which is God. Right now your good already **is** because completeness is. Right now Life already is. Healing is simply the experience of letting go of yesterday and embracing today. Today already is, perfection already is, God already is.

The experience of today is letting go of the hurts, the resentments, and the memories of yesterday. Potential is not yesterday, it is not tomorrow. Potential is the NOW. Our potential already is. It is God. Potential is being fully aware of Who and What you are and then using that self-awareness. What we give is what we receive, that is the law of life. But trying to be nice to everyone does not create health. Trying to give up a bad habit does not create health. The more you are aware of the habit, the more you try to be free of it, the more you maintain it, or, let us say, it maintains you. The approach to true and lasting health does not come about through staying out of drafts, putting on your rubbers when it rains, or eating a certain diet. All of these may be expressed as a result of a consciousness of Life, as we receive the inner instructions from the idea we are using, but they do not create health. Making someone comfortable at the body level does not create a healing consciousness. It simply makes him comfortable for the time being. If he does not do something new with his use of thought, if he is not involved with expressing his total Self, he will not be permanently healed.

It is Life that heals. Life is our experience as we are aware of it. This healing consciousness of Life cannot be developed by looking to any person, place, or thing as being cause to your experience. If you believe in the negative power of germs, then you are being controlled by this belief in the destructive action of germs. This belief takes you away from the awareness of Who and What you really are, and it is your experience. If you believe in God, the NOW, then you know that nothing can touch you which does not correspond with this Presence of perfection. Some people make diets their god, but no diet has ever created the awareness of

God, of Life. Fullness must be experienced in **every** area of life. The god of diet has only made these people believe more in body as being cause.

Through the awareness of life, of an idea of completeness, the intelligence which is within each idea you use reveals all that needs to be thought, said, and done. Diet is then no longer a god but a result of Life-awareness. Balance takes place and an inner intelligence reveals what needs to be eaten and establishes a state of mind that permits the food to be digested easily and rightly.

The way in which you use your thought always determines your experience. You can evolve at the level of the beliefs of the world. You can seek material success and achieve it, for you are still, after all, using your thought to produce an experience. But in choosing to think, create, and grow at the material level, you are going to have to react to others—you must then evolve at this "people" level. In terms of your experience of health, you can use your thought to bring you to the right doctors, the right diets, the right exercises, and all of the fads that are a part of the world experience. You can keep up with the Joneses, you can evolve for the purpose of status, for the purpose of satisfying the ego. Material success can very well be achieved in this way, but this is a far cry from moving forward at the level of Wholeness, at the level of God. In directing the law of mind at the level of people, things, and body, you must be involved with the time element that this way of life believes in, and there are very few instantaneous demonstrations at the level of world belief.

If you are experiencing illness and go to your practitioner for the purpose of being healed, you do not want to be involved with days, weeks, or perhaps months of a slow healing process. What you want is instantaneous healing. Putting on a bandage, some ointment or iodine, or having an operation is not going to bring about your healing today, for in doing so, you are only working at the body level. None of these bring you instantly in tune with the healing consciousness, although they may be a part of the process. The desire of anyone who suffers from some physical limitation should be to experience perfect health

NOW. There are those, of course, who want their illness, for it may be a way of getting attention; but in spiritual healing there must be the receptivity, the desire, for full and total healing. The Presence of God is a total idea of perfection that is in action in the present moment. In identifying with the Nowness of God, Its completeness, you must experience immediate healing, for where there is an awareness of God, there must be health. Where there is an awareness of God, there must be the experience of God, and God is total beingness now. Only at the level of God can there be a healing today. Your healing is today because where you are, God is. Not a part of It, but all of It. Not dribs and drabs of Life, but all of Life.

Within body there is no power. Within things there is no power. Body and things are results, they are not cause. Power only comes from awareness, from your use of thought. Thinking at the level of body maintains you in the limits of body. It does not free you to know the experience of wholeness. With the spiritual consciousness all negative manifestations must disappear, for where your attention is must be your experience. If your attention is upon that which knows only Life, there must be the experience of Life. If you believe that healing takes a certain length of time, then you are directing the law of mind at the body level, at the level of world belief, and this must be your experience. When you believe in time, you have your demonstration of time belief, therefore what you know is delay. Delay must be your demonstration because you are not applying the idea of God, of NOW, to your present experience. Is it possible to have a healing today? **Yes.** It depends, of course, upon your belief, upon your acceptance. To the degree that you believe in God, to that degree do you experience God.

Living in the Eternal Now means that you not only have your thought focused upon this moment, but upon what this moment really is. You are aware of the Presence, the Allness of God, right where you are NOW. God is a God of the now, not of yesterday. Not part of God, but all of God, is everywhere present at all times. In the Mind of God the time is always now and the idea is always the completeness of God.

The more completely you practice the Presence of God, the more you have your demonstrations, your healings, today. As you take this approach, your goals are fulfilled in a much shorter period of time than if you believe in a sequence and a necessary passage of time. You may be building a house and believe that it cannot be built in a day. But is that your goal? Your goal is to experience the fullness, the completeness of God as you right now; and you can still live, act, and express that fullness now, regardless of whether or not the house is fully constructed. To the degree that we go all the way with our thought, to that degree do we have our healing today.

It is our purpose in using the science of mind to always work with the "single eye." This is what treatment really is — to be eternally aware of that which already is. We must use our thought to know that everything we desire already is. If we can be aware of it in mind, then it is already so because the reality is always in mind. When you have the idea that as you treat or claim your goal and thus set the law of subconscious mind in motion, you will eventually have your demonstration, you are delaying your goal, or perhaps keeping it forever from you. It is the law of mind that whatever you believe, you experience. If you believe in your goal, your purpose, your healing, as being a NOW action, then it is. Jesus used this method of awareness, the practicing of the Presence, and instantaneous healings took place. Not only did this approach work for him, but he said, in essence, that if he could do it, so could anyone else who believed in the same way. Yes, even greater works did he claim for those who practiced the Presence, for whatever can be conceived in mind can be and is achieved. If, with the "single eye," we can conceive of instantaneous healing, then the law of mind must accept that belief and demonstrate it.

You should not be ashamed of making great claims upon mind. The greater the better. We are meant to live life on the grand scale, and we should dare to think boldly and dynamically, for this is our means to know life, to know God, to know ourselves. If instantaneous healing seems to be asking for too much, then you will never experience it. Healing is nothing more than a recognition of something that already is. In recognizing the presence of completeness, you are not asking for something that is impossible. It already IS. All we have to do is to help ourselves through complete acceptance.

It may seem very difficult when you are in the middle of a problem to take your attention completely away from what appears to be and to put it on that Presence wherein there is no problem. But because of the law of mind that what you give your attention to is instantly your experience, it is not difficult because you can always do something about your thought. The answer is never within the problem, it is always within the Presence of Life, of Truth, of God. Shifting your attention to a belief in wholeness is not ignoring the challenge, it is actually solving or being free of the problem. If you want to be free of the problem, the only effective thing you can do is to consciously readjust your point of attention to an idea that could not possibly include the problem. In putting your attention on Truth, on Wholeness, you also benefit by being free of any other aspect of limitation.

We find ourselves in problems only because we think at the level of effect, at the level of people and things, rather than at the level of Truth. There is certainly nothing wrong with people, in having them in our lives (in fact it is a necessity as well as a joy), but when we let them be cause to our experience rather than keeping our attention on our purpose in being, we are no longer free agents, we are no longer free to determine our own Divine destiny. Your healing does not come from people or what they can give to you. It comes from your consciousness of wholeness. People are meant to be in our lives in the right and ideal way, but this can only happen when we are first of all at one with the consciousness that is free of anger, resentment, anxiety, or fear. At the level of God no argument could ever take place. At the level of God there is nothing to defend or to justify. There is only something to know and to express. Each person in your world is very important—but not as cause.

Within each one of us there is a Total and Complete Self. Within each one of us is that consciousness which we call the Christ—God as you. It is a divine Center that is whole, absolutely perfect and pure.

There is a Self that has never made a mistake and never will. It may be covered over and hidden by countless beliefs in the opposite, but It is still there. We do not necessarily have to try to remove all of those layers of false beliefs, opinions, and memories of previous mistakes. This can take years and is not really very effective because they then have to be replaced with other opinions and beliefs. All we have to do is to consciously be aware of the Total Self, and It instantly is free to be our present experience. It is not something that is weak or powerless from disuse, for Its beingness has never ceased. It has always been Itself, but did not express Itself in our ego or human experience because our attention was elsewhere. It is Life Itself, and Life certainly never ceases to be just because we have a distorted concept of It. Treatment is for the purpose of being consciously aware of this Total Self, this individualization of God that each of us really is.

Each one of us was created out of the Whole, out of God; we were created in Its image and likeness. God is not a person, It is not body, It is not effect, It is not finite.

We have all been so busy living in the the world and being of the world that we have not taken the time to turn within to be aware of Who and What we really are. Our concept of God may have been given to us by someone else, and it may therefore resemble a distorted version of man. Being free of such an erroneous concept is our first task at hand. God is not man, God is not body, God is not that which is finite. It is Infinite or It would not be God, and so It cannot be brought to the level of body or even of definition. Whatever It is, we know that It is perfection, fullness, completeness, and that is good enough a concept to start with in the healing process.

Today the True Self is again being revealed—free of theology and doctrine. We are once more returning to the teachings of Jesus that have been all but ignored because of our worship of Jesus the man for nearly the past two thousand years. It is the purpose of each one of us to awaken to the nature of our True Being—to use our thought to be constantly aware of Who and What we really are. In this awakening to the nature of the Self, problems and limitations cease to be our experience. We are once more individualizations of God, of unlimited Being. In our awareness that we are individualizations of Life, of God, and therefore individualizations of fullness and completeness, the law of mind is accepting our use of thought and is bringing into our individual experience all that God, all that completeness, is. There is nothing wrong in treating for healing, or for the demonstrations of all that we desire, but let us first of all use our thought to recognize Who and What we really are, and then this fullness will automatically fill every area of our lives. Our very experience is immediately harmonized to correspond with the Perfect Being that each of us really is. In other words, instantaneous healing.

Your healing is today when you rise in your use of thought, in consciousness, so that you transcend in your attention all that is visible. You go beyond what is seen and heard in the outer world and touch the full recognition of the Total Being that you really are, that God is as you. Health is an active awareness of Life, of that which is whole and complete, whether you call it God or something else. Health is being fully aware of Who and What you really are and expressing this awareness. You may say this is not treatment, but all awareness is directing the law of mind. Awareness is treatment because it is still an action in mind, an activity of thought. It is more effective, however, to know what you are doing, to do it deliberately so that you can consciously go beyond your present level of experience. In this way you also make sure that you do not admit into your consciousness ideas presented to you from the world.

In order to fulfill your purpose, your goals, you must keep your attention on the purpose, the goal. Let the law of mind take care of the details. When you become busy with manipulating people, forcing something to happen, or trying to get something from someone, you are no no longer at the level of God. Always keep your awareness upon the Presence so that It can create through you, so that your level of thought is such that God can think by means of you. Your healing can be today only when you are at one with that which brings everything into harmony with Itself. Body does not heal, people do not heal, and you certainly can never force a healing to take place. It is only God, Life, that heals, simply by going right on being Itself. When you are in tune with this Infinite Thinker, you always have all that you need. When you are at one with your Total Self, your every thought directs the law of mind in such a way that you can experience nothing less than God.

When you are aware of Who and What you really are, you can look out upon the world and truly know that any seeming limitation does not really exist. What seems to be is merely the result of someone's using a limited idea. That's all it is, a limited use of thought. A thinking individual has separated himself in his use of thought from the Total Being that he really is, and has thus directed the law of mind in an incomplete way. Such mental action must manifest as poverty, disease, loneliness, unhappiness, or some other condition that does not permit someone to live completely. When you know that you are the Beingness of God, you cannot possibly think in a small, mediocre, or negative way. The consciousness of God simply does not function in that way. In seeing yourself as being whole, complete, God as you, this way of thought must fill every area of your experience with all that reflects this wholeness, this completeness.

The truth is that the kingdom of wholeness, of life, of God, does not have to be created. It already is. It has always been and always will be. This kingdom is already within each one of us. It is within our thought, within our consciousness. Because this is so, we can always turn consciously to that center of wholeness and be aware of Its fullness if we so choose. It is never God that grows by means of us. God can never be more complete than It already is. It is our awareness that must grow and expand. In this awareness we have our healing. Your recognition of God is your experience of God. God is not a person, a place, or a thing. It is this completeness, this awareness of Total Being. It is a way of thought. Your healing takes place today when you become at one with the concept that God as you is perfect, complete, whole. You do this consciously —through treatment, through your awareness. Your wholeness already is because God already is. Your freedom already is because God already is—right now, right where you are. It is the entirety of Itself always and everywhere present. Too many of us try to make our healings take place when perfection already is. We try to force God to do something and to be something that It has always been, is now, and always will be. With this type of mental manipulation it is no wonder that the treatment cannot work, for the individual who does this is, in essence, saying "My good is not already so. I have to cause God to make it happen." The subconscious mind can only accept the orders we give it in the way that we give them. If we don't believe that our full expression of life is already so, then this limited belief is our experience. Our experience is always the demonstration of our level of belief.

Do not use your thought to deny the appearance, for in doing so you are still giving your attention to the appearance. Where your attention is must be your experience. In denying something, you are really emphasizing what you are denying because you are giving your attention to the problem. Treatment is for the purpose of lifting your thought to touch the consciousness of God. Even in just knowing a

Truth, or in saying an affirmation, you are not using your thought greatly enough. What we want is to be at one with that Center of Total Being within each of us—God Itself. What we need is the realization of the Presence of God. God as you, God as all. The today healing takes place through the awareness of God—not just the idea of health. An affirmation that says "I am free of all debt" still focuses your attention on debt, and it does not bring you to the level of thought that is only aware of Its fullness, that cannot comprehend the idea or experience of indebtedness. The today healing can take place only through completely letting go of the problem and identifying totally with that which will fill every area of life with Its perfection, not just take care of one thing. When you touch this level of thought through your treatment, you realize that there is only God AS ALL. You also automatically know this fullness for every person who comes to your use of thought. When you reach this point, you are on your way into the growing experience of God.

If you are thinking through the Law of God, the law of wholeness, then the law of mind must bring into your life the manifestations of this way of thought. Your experience always equals the state of your awareness, the idea that you are using. Nothing more, nothing less. Using your treatment to be healed in the right way, at the right time, after a certain period of time, is not going to bring about a today healing. Only a full acceptance of the NOW will do this. Your treatments must always be the recognition of the fullness of God, **all** of the aspects of God. Your treatments should never give attention to a problem, nor should your thought claim only a part of God. In the awareness of Wholeness, there is no such thing as a person with a problem. There is only Wholeness individualized. The perfection of God is poured into all areas of Being and brings into balance whatever appears not to be whole. If you feel that you need to treat for health, you must still go beyond that single aspect of God and claim all of God so that the fullness of God will be brought into whatever else is required for the full experience of freedom. The Total Self should be in expression always. This will automatically result in being in the right job, in experiencing prosperity, health and love. In treating just for the right job, you

are forgetting the most important ingredi-
ent—your Total Self. The law of attraction
always brings to you what you are, what
you are expressing. Your Total Self does
not express Itself just while you are at
work. It goes on expressing Itself at all
times, in all that you do, and thus draws to
Itself through the law of attraction all that
It requires for Its expression.

To know the truth about Life, about God,
and yet to think of that truth as being something separate from yourself or from anyone else is really to deny God. If God is,
It IS. God is that wholeness that is everywhere present at all times—not a part of Itself, but all of Itself. Otherwise It would
not be God. If you do not believe that each
person in your world is an individualization
of God, then you do not believe in God.
God is everywhere present. God must be
where you are, It must be where everyone
is, and It must be there as the completeness of Itself. There is no such thing as a
part of God.

To say that you are getting better and
better each and every day is to deny the
wholeness of God, to deny God Itself. All
of God is where you are NOW. If you are

treating for someone else, you must be aware of the wholeness of God—the wholeness of God as the wholeness of yourself and as the wholeness of this individual, for it is all God. As you know the Presence of God, you must know it not only for yourself, but for ALL, otherwise you are trying to deal in the parts of God, and there are no parts. God is, above all, wholeness. In dealing with God there is no such thing as partness, halfness, or discrimination. You cannot say that God is health, but not prosperity, or one person, but not another. God is ALL.

Your treatment, your realization, your awareness, can be accomplished in a moment, a few minutes, or it may take all day, depending upon how long it takes you to arrive at that level of awareness wherein there is the sensing of this wholeness, this completeness. Actually this awareness is something that should be going on all day long anyway, not just when we are experiencing a problem. We are always thinking, and it is our responsibility to make sure that the ideas we use are **always** in tune with the Total Self. Our thought should be a deliberate, yet spontaneous, action in mind. Memorizing a treatment that someone else has written is not as effective as one you give yourself, in your own words. The most effective treatment in our own experience is always the one we ourselves give, one that springs from our own individual use of thought, one that is spontaneous. You can read a daily treatment, and this is fine. But it should be just a beginning of what you do with your own thought. It merely points the way, and you take it from there. Imitation can never be as successful or as full as spontaneous self-expression.

Inspiration always comes from the need of the moment, not from yesterday's treatment, or even from yesterday's healing. All that you require for full self-expression must come from the now. Now is where your healing is because in the NOW is where God is. In the NOW perfection is. When you take into your today your failures or even your successes of yesterday, you are cutting yourself off from that which is being expressed by the new, which is the now. NOW is all you have. Most of us, in our use of thought, cannot comprehend this. We cling to yesterday and look forward to tomorrow. But **today** is where the healing is. God already is—NOW. All that you need to know in order to succeed in your present purpose is yours this moment within the now consciousness of Universal Mind, which is always geared for the activity of today. Inspiration always comes when you are spontaneously self-activated, when you seek to draw out of your Self all that you need. Treatment is for the purpose of turning within to these inner resources of the nowness of God and opening wide the floodgates of self-expression.

It is the law of mind that what we give our attention to we always experience. The more we talk about, think about, and react to a problem, the longer it is going to be in our experience. The more that we refer to the completeness of the Self, the wholeness of God individualized as each one of us, the more rightly we direct the law of mind and thus have our today healing. Give all power in your thought to the totality of God, the Whole Self, the fullness of the purpose, goal, or any idea that you are using, and this must become visible in your body, your experience, in every area of your life. Your healing is today when you put your attention on what you ARE rather than upon what you were. Your problem is not what you are, but what you think you are, which, in turn, is based upon what you were. The problem is a result of what you have already thought and ex- expressed. Let go if it. Be deliberately aware of the nowness of your True Self, the nowness of God, and you must be free of the problem. Your healing is today.

Those who first discover the power of mind, the law of mind, usually seek to use mind in order to be healed of some par- ticular disease, some limitation that is get- ting in the way of the full, rich life. It can be used for that purpose, to be sure. It can be used to bring whatever you desire into your life. What we really want, how- ever, is a lasting healing, a total harmoniz- ing of our outer experience with our inner Reality, not just a stopgap measure. The initial healings are very good because they prove to us that the science of mind works. But in the goal of instantaneous and last- ing healing we must go further and direct the law of mind in a greater way. The goal should always be the awareness of whole- ness, the awareness of Who and What you really ARE. It must be the realization of God. When you have this, you automatically have everything, for then this way of thought makes every area of your life complete at the mental, physical, and experience levels. This way of thought creates all that is needed. Not only does It balance everything, but since God already is, the law of NOWNESS instantly does Its work.

Instead of treating each finger, one at a time, you can treat the whole hand. But you should go further. Instead of treating the hand, treat the whole limb. Even this is a beginning. Instead of treating the limb, treat the whole body. But since there is no reality in body, since body is but a reflection of the consciousness that is using it, let us, instead, treat the consciousness. Not our own individual consciousness, but the consciousness of God, of which we are an outlet, an individualization.

Wholeness only knows wholeness. It cannot know partness. That which is complete cannot be aware of any concept of incompleteness. Incompleteness is simply a result of not being aware of completeness. Using our thought correctly is all a matter of focus, of awareness. In our treatments many of us are so concerned with the various aspects of an apparent limitation that we cannot let that which is complete flow through us. This is why so many many treatments are not demonstrated. We are directing the law of mind at the level of the limitation, at the level of time and space, instead of contacting that which knows no time or space. God can only understand completeness. It only knows Its completeness NOW. You cannot contact that level of completeness and then tell completeness how to be complete. It already IS. The intelligence within completeness knows how to manifest that completeness in whatever way is required to demonstrate completeness. God cannot be told to fight someone or to make something happen in a certain way. It is our purpose to keep our attention upon the goal, upon the purpose, upon Who and What we are, and to let the intelligence of God take care of the details. In telling God how to be full, how to be whole, we are actually denying an acceptance of God. We are denying God Its true nature. This way of thought does not work because nothing can or will diminish God. The only thing that is diminished in this approach is our experience of God because we are not permitting all of It to come through into our awareness and experience.

You will never have peace of mind or your healing today if the purpose of your treatment is to cause something to happen to someone, or if you are fighting a problem with your thought. You only have peace of mind when there is no conflict. You only have peace of mind when you realize that your good already is, that your healing has already taken place, that you are **already** whole. You only have peace of mind when there is but one Source in your use of thought, the Source which is already whole and complete—God. God as you. Peace of mind means releasing people, things, and results, and letting the law of consciousness do its creative work. We become so involved with people that we fail to realize it is our purpose to be involved with God, with our own inner resources and wholeness. The people who come into your world are there as the result of your thought, the result of consciousness. Your experience with them is always the experience of your Self, your way of thought.

Your healing with them can take place only when you release everyone in your world and instead are at one with your Whole Self. There will always be people in your world because the law of attraction is going to demonstrate them. They are always there to help you experience your consciousness and not to be cause to your experience. You are in their experience for the very same reason. Be involved with the wholeness within them and not their behavior—be aware of the perfection within them, not what they say or do.

Your thought, then, must be used for the purpose of the realization of the Whole and Perfect Being that you already are. To try to direct God to do something for you is not the way to experience wholeness. To use your thought to be aware that you already are complete, that your good already is, is the only way. Your healing is today when you reach in your thought and feeling the realization of the Presence. Your healing is today when you sense that It is where you are, that It is you. Your healing is today when you reach that level of thought where it is actually God thinking by means of you. We can all do this. There are none who cannot if they sincerely try. It means letting go of all that is visible. It means letting go of person, place, and thing as cause to your experience. It means letting go of yesterday and tomorrow. It means being involved with God rather than the details. It means letting go of ego and deliberately BEING the Presence of God.

ALL YOU HAVE IS NOW

WHEN YOU ARE INVOLVED with your thought in how something is going to take place, the best way to make something work, you cannot function creatively. In the first place, when you do this, you do not see your goal or desire as already being accomplished. Your attention is so involved with the process that the idea cannot be demonstrated. The process says that it is not already so. We know that the subconscious mind takes whatever we believe in and produces it in our experience. This law is infallible; it has been proven over and over again. When we first discover this, it is exciting to prove it for ourselves. Too many times, however, we become involved in how it is going to happen, when, and where. This is absolutely none of our business. As we move along in our spiritual growth, we discover that the fastest way to let something take place is to give our full attention to the goal, to the purpose, to the idea being used, and to see it as already being so. We stop giving our attention to how it is happening, or to how it is going to happen, or to any mechanical or automatic process.

Never fear. The idea that you are using is already directing this law of mind. That's all that you need to know—what it is that you are now thinking, now giving, now expressing. You cannot give a treatment and then sit back and wait for something to happen. Your today thought produces your today experience. Whatever happens today comes about because of what you are thinking and doing right now—not because of what you did yesterday. If you believe that yesterday is cause to today, you will always be looking back to yesterday instead of giving your full attention to today. Your experience of this present moment is a result of your now attitude, your now idea. In other words, you must not carry either yesterday or tomorrow around in your today use of thought. You may be preparing a meal in the early part of the day that is going to be eaten in the evening, but you are still doing it right now. You don't have to worry about how the ingredients are going to blend or about what happens when you put it in the oven or pan. All you have to do is keep your goal in mind, follow the recipe, which is not a process but an activity of self-expression, and let the idea carry you forward. As you are aware of what you are now doing, as you are involved with this self-expression of the present moment, you have all of the enthusiasm, energy, and joy that you need. If you are afraid that it might not turn out right, or that you might receive some criticism, you begin to falter. Or if you think about all of the things that you have to do later while you are in the act of doing, you will become anxious, tired, and begin resisting the whole idea.

As you see it as already being accomplished, or have the complete picture in mind, then the idea unfolds easily and rightly. When you see yourself as having to do it all, having to figure everything out beforehand, you either stop before you get started or become discouraged along the way because you are directing the law of mind in a limited way. In essence you are being very egotistical. You are saying that you know more than God does. When you let go of ego and learn to trust that Inner Self, which is an individualization of God, what you are doing is a now, concentrated experience because it is the goal, the purpose now unfolding, and all that needs to be done right now is done. In seeing the desire, the goal or purpose, as a now idea, you know that it is already so. In knowing this, it IS. The law of mind cannot deny it. The moment that you become involved with the process, you have a problem.

There is an Intelligence within each one of us, and within the idea we are using, that knows what to do and how to do it so that whatever idea we are using is fulfilled. We not only need to know what it is that we desire to experience, but we also need to know Who and What we are. We do not need to know how all of this is to be demonstrated. If we try to find out, we have changed our goal, our point of attention, and we are then going in the wrong direction. The "how" must be left to the intelligence of Universal Subconscious Mind. As you learn to let go of yesterday, you stop living on borrowed time and you begin to live out of the vast, infinite Within. Let us call it "God as you." In doing this, you eliminate delay, you free yourself from the limitations of yesterday and of the anxieties about tomorrow. You are thus able to BE. Should you recall your mistakes of yesterday or the way that others behaved in your dealings with them in the past, you will say "no" to doing something in a certain way when you are instructed to do so from within. If you are involved with the voice of yesterday, you will not be able to hear the voice of Today speaking. God is the voice of TODAY. Your Whole and Total Self is the voice of today. We need new and greater ideas, not sameness. No matter how great yesterday was, it does not fit within the purpose of today.

The more that you can give your conscious attention to what you **are** rather than to what you were, the more you can have your instantaneous healing or demonstration. In BEING, your unlimited potential can come into active expression. In living in the past to any degree, you are just about ignoring your potential. On the other hand, when you are consciously aware of this idea of wholeness that you are right now, the law of mind must accept this way of thought as it does any other way of thought. It is ridiculous to delay your good even by a moment when you can have it all right now.

Within each of us is Infinity because within each one of us, no matter how hidden it may be, is the idea of Infinity. Within each one of us is an idea of absolute perfection and completeness, regardless of how much it is disguised. Within each one of us is that Whole Being we call God. As we are aware of this vastness, this totality of Being, we automatically demonstrate all of which we are aware. What you have already accomplished can only get in the way of your greater use of thought. Your fears, resentments, anxieties do not belong in the total way of thought that each of us can learn to use. We can be aware of this wholeness only when we take our attention away from yesterday and tomorrow and put it on what we ARE and upon what we are now doing. As you release yesterday and tomorrow, you stop living on borrowed time. You are able to BE.

In the action of doing, in living in the eternal now, you find time for everything. In the now there is no hurry, there is no fear. There is only the creative action of a Total Self that knows what to do and how to do it. In the now there is no fear because your attention is upon expressing, doing, and not upon what might or might not take place. Every idea that you use carries within it the intelligence of the Universe to fulfill this idea. Take your attention away and you instantly begin experiencing something else. Keeping your attention upon what you ARE rather than upon what you were permits the now idea to draw into your experience whatever that idea requires.

You do not need more of yesterday. You need the new, the more, the better. You need the NOW. As you become involved with the action of the idea, the goal or purpose, the answer is already there. Action is NOW. It is in doing, being, that you discover Who and What you are. Therefore, all that you need to know IS right now. It is within the idea you are now using. Make that idea one of completeness, and you have enough to fill every area of your life with infinite good.

When you approach life from the outer world of form, intellect, process, you find yourself involved with a time sequence. You discover yourself giving your attention to one step at a time. But in the inner kingdom of the Whole Self, the whole idea, it is already so. YOU ALREADY ARE. GOD ALREADY IS. Instantaneous healing can take place only when you have the whole idea in mind and see it as already being so. If you are in tune with the idea, then you are in tune with everything else, for the idea is what you need. The rest is automatic. In Mind there is no time. In Mind all already is, or you would not be able to be aware of it. Time only exists at the human or world level of thought. The more you are concerned with the hours of the day, the days of the week, the months of the year, the more you are trying to divide your being up into segments. Our thought must pull everything together, not send it out into different directions. God is already complete. Each of us is an individualization of God, an individualization of completeness. The only reason this does not seem to be so is that our awareness of this truth is not complete. Most of us are using ideas or concepts that fragmentize rather than unify. Be aware of the concept of wholeness and wholeness must be your experience. Believe it and it is so. Know, and you experience your knowingness.

It is our challenge, our opportunity, as we move forward in our use of the law of mind, to grow and expand in our use of thought. Now that we know that our beliefs become form, we must expand our beliefs and choose greater ideas into which to pour them. If you believe in delay, time sequence, then this must be your experience. The law is the law. If, on the other hand, you build your belief in instantaneous healing, this, too, must be your experience. In trying to figure out how and when something should be done, you become involved with the process rather than with the whole idea. The process thus gets in the way.

The concept of speed reading is to learn to take in at a glance as much of the page as is possible so that you get the full picture all at once, rather than just one word following another until you get the whole sentence or idea. When you look at a room, you see the entire room, all of its furnishings, every detail of it, in just a glance. You don't figure out how it was furnished or when, and you don't need to know how long it took to be completed. You see it now and you can use it now—all of it, if you so desire, or as much as you need. As you train yourself to look at the whole page in speed reading, you can get the whole picture at once and thereby can fly from page to page. You are filling your consciousness with whole ideas in a moment. So it is in your use of thought. See completeness within every moment, within every activity, within every experience, and this way of thought instantly becomes form. Consciously choose to see the completeness of the goal, of your Self, and this is what you must experience.

You do not need to know all of the steps along the way before you start out. What you need is the whole idea, the answer. In order to accomplish all that needs to be done as it needs to be done, turn in your use of thought to the whole idea. Turn to the Inner Kingdom of your Whole Self, and everything flows smoothly. The action of BEING your SELF takes place, and it is the right experience. Knowing the whole idea now, produces the whole idea now, and you have your instantaneous healing.

It is always the purpose of each one of us to live fully, and this means giving all of ourselves to the present moment. This means using the Total idea of your Complete Self at all times. It does not mean saving your self-expression for another time. You cannot say "I'll express love tomorrow afternoon at three o'clock and energy the following day." What about right now? This very moment needs the expression of love. This present moment needs the release of energy in creative ways. This moment needs the intelligence of the Universe. You have it all. It is where you are right now. It is within the idea of your Complete Self. God as you. You are only living on borrowed time when you try to save your Self for tomorrow or go back into yesterday for a comparison, a resentment, or a fond look at what you have successfully completed. All you need is in the present moment. All you really have is the NOW. You only have as you live, as you give. You cannot give yesterday. Giving is not a promise, so you cannot give the future. You can only give what you are. What you **are** is where your potential is. What you **are** is where God is. What you **are** is NOW.

Each of us has a purpose in being. We each have a purpose in this day, in the present moment. You cannot fulfill this purpose when you are rehearsing either yesterday or tomorrow. It is true that we all need goals in order to go beyond yesterday. We always need a focus of attention. But every goal must be seen as a now action, a now experience. If you are treating for a new and more beautiful home, that idea must be seen as already so, and you must live as though it were so right now. Living out of your Whole Self will produce not only the more beautiful home, but whatever else is required for that concept to be experienced. We must live that purpose, that goal. Act as though it were so, and in the beingness of it, you have it. You can only have what you are. In order to demonstrate more, you must first of all be more aware of Who and What you really are. Take that idea of completeness. Live it. Let it use you. Be that idea in action, and the law of attraction instantly creates the opportunity for that fullness to be expressed. BEING is all you have.

The only moment in which you can be secure is in the moment of Being. In BEING, you are in charge. In BEING, nothing can happen to you that is not in accord with your Self-awareness and your Self-expression. Your fears are not the action of being. They are centered upon the future, tomorrow. Your angers and resentments are not the action of BEING. They are attachments to what has already happened. You cannot afford either yesterday or tomorrow. What you need is today. What you need is to be your Self—that idea of perfection and completeness which you already are. In your purpose of being, you live life fully, honestly—with love, joy, enthusiasm, success, and unlimited power because in BEING, your Whole and Total Self is in action right now. It must manifest as fullness in every area of your life.

If you want to be free, to have your healing today, you must stop living on borrowed time. Stop treating for things that will take place in the future, stop living in the past, and start using your thought to BE. All that you need is here, NOW, TODAY. In thinking and living out of the fullness of today, you are always prepared for all challenges as they come along. You see each one as an opportunity to use your inner resources in a greater way when you are aware of what you ARE, when you live completely in today. Instead of rehearsing for tomorrow, make the most of today. When you do this, all that you are is poured into all that you do. Your active awareness of the completeness that you are causes you to live and give greatly, to use your money and time wisely so that you are always a concept of fullness, a concept of balance. Investing is a today action. But putting everything away for a rainy day—your goals, purpose, talents, abilities, as well as all of your money—keeps you from growing. Unless your talents are used and stretched, they are no longer yours. There are those, too, who spend all of their money as soon as it comes in, but they are not using wisdom, they are not using the inner intelligence that will permit them to invest, to produce more and better. The more that you express your total Self, the more you realize that there are even greater resources of intelligence, energy, power, and love within you. Spend your Self appropriately and you will not waste a moment.

When you sit around just waiting for something to happen, time goes by very slowly indeed. When you are filled with dread for some future event that you would like to escape but know is coming, then time seems to pass very quickly. But when you are involved with BEING, in using your highest and best at all times, then there is no sense of time, there is only the fullness of the eternal now. Life is the eternal now, for Life is always action, that which is now taking place. In being involved with living, you have all that Life is—health, wealth, peace of mind, and love. It is our purpose, yours and mine, to always live out of a sense of fullness. GOD IS NOW. I AM NOW.

Instead of treating for things, for something to happen, treat for ideas. Because of the law of mind, when you make your command upon Mind for great ideas, great ideas are what you receive. The ideas that you accept, believe in, and use are the ideas that you experience. You don't have to accept every thought that comes to you. You have the freedom to choose only those which produce the good that you desire, those which help you to express your Ideal Self at all times. Choose the greatest and most complete ideas that you can. They are the ones that really pay off. Include in each one the essence of NOW. "It is already so." Instantaneous healing is no accident. If you believe in the nowness of each goal, purpose, and idea that you use, they are demonstrated now.

In the present moment there is absolutely nothing to be afraid of. Fear is tomorrow. Since you can only live one moment at a time, and since you can do something about the moment that you are now experiencing, then you can eliminate all fear from your experience. You can learn to live in the now. Right where you are, you are in the middle of all the life there is. Right where you are, you are in the middle of all of the intelligence and power there is. Be aware of this moment and all that it contains and it is yours. Within this moment is God. Within this moment is a way of thought. Within this moment is a Presence. Within this moment is ALL.

Begin right where you are. Begin in this moment. Begin with an idea. An idea of completeness. Specialize it in any way that you desire, but let it be as complete as you can possibly imagine. That which you desire to experience or demonstrate already is, or you would not be able to be aware of this desire. Within Mind all is complete. All you need is an idea. The law of mind is automatic. The result or effect must take place as long as you are at one with the cause, the thought. Activate your goal by knowing that it is already so. It **is** already so in Mind. Then put it into expression, into action. Act as though it were so, and in the action of it, it **is** so. In the activity of that purpose, that idea, there are no deadlines. It is already so. You have all the time that you need when you are using all of your powers now. Live out of the fullness of the idea that you already are, and you accomplish all that needs to be done as it needs to be done. Nothing can stop this from taking place except your taking your attention away from Who and What you are and putting it upon what you want to get, acquire, or do in the future.

There is no tomorrow. In putting off until tomorrow the action of today, you are forever separating your today good from your experience. NOW is all there is. As the challenge, the opportunity, arrives, face it by being at one with all that you are. Your Whole Self already is. There is that within you that knows what to do. It is the intelligence of the idea of your Whole Self. This intelligence knows how to do it. It is completeness as you—God as you.

When you live in the moment fully, as your Total Self, there is time for play as well as for work. It is all the same thing. It is all the expression of Self-Awareness. All of Truth, all of Power, all of Life, are in this present moment and are yours to use, regardless of what you are doing. Be aware of them and you instantly become the outlet of them. As you are involved with life, with using your inner resources, you are that which is ageless. Living has never caused anyone to age or to die. Living can only produce the effects of life. What many people call "living" is not that at all, for they mean the burdens, the catastrophes, the anxieties, fears, and negatives as well as the good. But Life has none of these negative qualities within It. Life is full, complete, total, always. It is that which is ever new, fresh, alive. Living in either yesterday or tomorrow, holding back the fullness of Self-expression, is what causes anyone to age, to grow old. Pain is yesterday, fear is tomorrow. God is today. Life is today.

When you live in today, every tension that you may have acquired from trying to force or will something to take place leaves you, and you discover that every moment is filled with all that you need as you need it. This is a result of BEING. In BEING, you take charge of your thought. You use it for awareness, to awaken within your consciousness all that you already are and always will be. With awareness of Who and What you are, you open wide to experience an infinite being that already is. It is God as you.

If you see yourself as being the process of "becoming," you will never experience that which you desire to become. Only in BEING do you demonstrate your good. You can never "become" successful or happy, healthy or wealthy. You can only BE. In seeking health, wealth, or happiness, you are in essence saying that none of these are already yours. You direct subconscious mind to thus ever keep them from you. They elude you because you can only have what you are or believe yourself to be. All is a state of BEING. What you are going to be is of no use to you now. Only what you are.

When you live out of the present moment, today, your sense of fullness can only expand and grow. Being free of the resentments of yesterday and the fears of tomorrow results in peace of mind. There is a serenity and an enthusiasm that are necessary to live creatively, to think construc- tively, to be able to hear the inner voice of Infinite Wisdom. When the channel, your awareness, is clogged with anxiety or an- ger, you cannot receive the ideas of suc- cess and completeness that you need. You receive only something that will feed the anxiety or the anger. A decision that is made out of fear will not be the right one for success, nor will one that is based upon yesterday. You and I are not here to repeat ourselves, to relive yesterday. We are here to grow and to expand in our self-aware- ness, and we cannot do so when our atten- tion is straying away from all that we ARE right now.

When you are living out of this present moment, not only is your healing taking place right now, but you are also giving your full attention to whatever you are now doing. There is no division in your atten- tion. Every thought, every atom of your Be- ing, is focused upon what you are, what you are doing, and this more dynamic and com- plete sense of awareness is directing the law of mind more clearly, more definitely, so that your demonstration can take place now. In giving or expressing in a more complete way, a more focused way, you must receive in a more complete and focused way. It is the individual who does not concentrate who never gets anything done. Why? Because his use of thought is going in a thousand different directions — he doesn't really know where he is or where he is going. If you don't recognize your purpose and don't put all of your attention and energies into it, that purpose will never be fulfilled.

When you are in tune with this moment, you are in charge. When you are in control, you know what it is that you are handling. The person who has self-confidence knows Who and What he is, he knows where he is going. He is dealing with the known, the now, not the unknown, the future. It is the self-confident individual who succeeds because he is a state of mind that is free. He is not bound by something that might or might not take place. He is busy expressing himself, his Whole Self. He is expressing a known quantity. Self-confidence is born out of the now, whereas anxiety is born out of a sense of incompleteness. Only in realizing that you **already** are a total individualization of God can you succeed in all that you do. Only in knowing Who and What you are can you express your Self with ease, joy, enthusiasm. In doing this, you must succeed. The law of cause and effect must create the right conditions, opportunities, and experiences for this self-confidence to flourish.

In your living in the eternal now as the completeness that you are, you always get things done. There is no procrastination. Because your attention is focused, you accomplish more, and you do whatever you do more creatively. When you are living in the now, in today, not only do you have your healing today, but life is now an exhilarating and exciting experience. You cannot possibly be depressed when your attention is upon what you ARE, upon what God is as you right now. You can only afford to live in the present, in today. Use your thought to accomplish the goal of BEING. In doing this, you will be astonished by your own self-discovery, by your vast inner resources, by your capacity and ability to succeed. Living in the now puts the full responsibility on your Inner Self, and thereby you discover your genius.

Your healing is today. This Is The Beginning!